SALVE REGINA

AMDG

Salve Regina

*The Rosary and other Prayers
illustrated from the Libraries
at Stonyhurst College*

*Compiled by
Charles Graffius & Edward Thomson*

2007
ST OMERS PRESS
Stonyhurst

All the illustrations in this book are from
the Libraries and Collections at Stonyhurst College.
Further information about these can be obtained by writing to the
Curator, Stonyhurst College, Clitheroe, Lancashire BB7 9PZ.

All Bible quotations are from
The Jerusalem Bible

First published in April 2007
by St Omers Press
3-9 Cripps Road, Cirencester, GL7 1HN

© 2007 Stonyhurst College

All rights reserved. No part of this publication may be reproduced,
stored in a retrieval system, or transmitted in any form or by any means, electronic,
mechanical, photocopying or otherwise, without the prior
permission of the copyright holder.

CIP data for this title are available
from the British Library

Printed in China

ISBN 978-0-9553592-1-7

Contents

7
INTRODUCTION

11
PRAYING THE ROSARY

13
INTRODUCTORY PRAYERS

17
THE JOYFUL MYSTERIES

29
THE SORROWFUL MYSTERIES

41
THE GLORIOUS MYSTERIES

53
THE MYSTERIES OF LIGHT

65
PRAYERS AFTER THE ROSARY

67
PRAYERS FROM PRIMERS

83
STONYHURST COLLEGE COLLECTIONS

96
LIST OF ILLUSTRATIONS

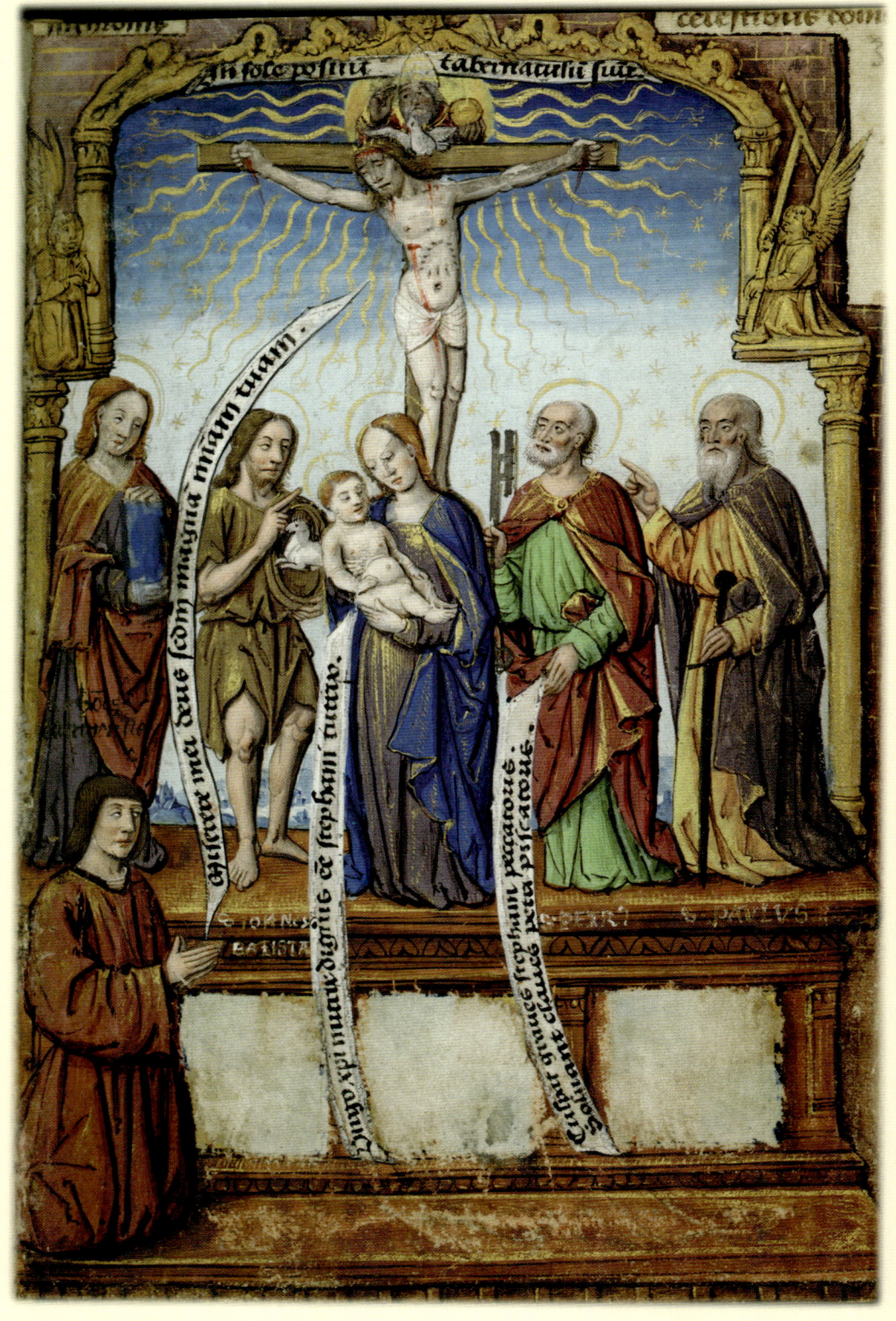

Introduction

THE ROSARY IS A FORM OF CATHOLIC prayer in use from ancient times, combining the simplicity of repetition with the profundity of meditation. The person saying the Rosary uses the rhythm of the recurring short prayers to set up a kind of background music, creating the mood and theme for contemplating the mystery that is being pondered.

For many people the Rosary provides the ideal focus on the central events of the life of Jesus Christ, and his work in our redemption: his birth, his public life, his sufferings and death, and his ascent to life and glory. These are the central themes of the scriptures, to be seen in their full depth by the Christian disciple.

For a long time the Rosary was made up of three sets of five Mysteries: those concerned with the coming of Jesus, called the Joyful Mysteries, ones about his suffering and death – the Sorrowful Mysteries – and a set on his Resurrection triumph and its consequences, known as the Glorious Mysteries. In 2002, Pope John Paul II introduced a further set of five Mysteries called the 'Mysteries of Light', dealing with the public life and miracles of Jesus, including the institution of the Eucharist.

Because the prayer consists largely of Hail Maries, the focus on the mysteries of Christ is seen from the point of view of Mary, mother and disciple of Jesus. The New Testament points out that she is involved at the crucial events of his life: his birth, of course, but also his first miracle and his death on the Cross. And Mary is shown at the heart of the early Christian community awaiting the coming of the Holy Spirit at Pentecost. Pope John Paul II described praying the Rosary as *contemplating, with Mary, the face of Christ.*

The way in which the Rosary is said can be very flexible. Some would simply say one decade, consisting of an Our Father, ten Hail Maries (hence the term 'decade') and a Glory Be to the Father. This would take just a couple of minutes. Most would see a standard Rosary as made up of five decades, one for each of the five Mysteries in a set, and would aim therefore to cover five of the Mysteries each day, completing the total twenty Mysteries over four days. A few enthusiasts might say the entire twenty decades in one session! It can be useful to introduce the prayer with a carefully selected scripture reading that describes the Mystery being contemplated. In communal recitations it may be appropriate to begin and end with a hymn.

The beauty and depth of this wonderful ancient way of prayer is neatly shown in the present volume. In using it the reader will be conscious of an attachment to one of the great ages of faith, when sincere and simple people lived their Christian religion with minimal schooling, but found genuine comfort and meaning from the regular practice of saying the Rosary. To many such people the possession of a Book of Hours was a vital aid to their spiritual life: the elaborate calligraphy reminded them of the great value of the inspired Word of God, whilst the highly symbolic pictures gave them a ready access to the profound truths of religion. It is to be hoped that this publication will enable men and women today to gain insight and depth in saying the Rosary, and in other forms of Christian prayer.

John Twist SJ
Chaplain, Stonyhurst College

Praying the Rosary

THE PRAYERS OF THE ROSARY ARE divided into the Joyful, Sorrowful and Glorious Mysteries, and more recently the Mysteries of Light. Each Mystery meditates on five events in the life of Jesus or Our Lady. This book presumes that the Rosary will be recited communally, or within the family – if you are praying alone then simply say all the prayers and responses.

Start the Rosary by making the Sign of the Cross, and then say the *Glory Be to the Father* and *Apostles' Creed* (p. 13), while holding the crucifix at the end of the rosary. Then say the *Our Father* on the next single bead, followed by three *Hail Maries* on the group of three beads, then *Glory Be* on the last single bead (p. 15). Decide which set of Mysteries you wish to pray, read the Gospel quote associated with it, and then move on to the first decade of the Mystery. Holding the medal which joins the circle of beads to the crucifix, recite the *Our Father*. For the ten *Hail Maries* which follow, use the group of ten beads, finishing the Mystery with a *Glory Be* on the next single bead; this bead also serves for the *Our Father* starting the next decade. Finish by reciting the *Prayers after the Rosary* (p. 65).

Introductory Prayers

All: In the name of the Father and of the Son and of the Holy Spirit. Amen.

Leader: O God, come to our aid.

All: O Lord make haste to help us.

Leader: Glory be to the Father, and to the Son and to the Holy Spirit.

All: As it was in the beginning, is now and ever shall be, world without end. Amen.

All: I believe in God the Father almighty, creator of heaven and earth; and in Jesus Christ, his only Son, Our Lord; who was conceived by the Holy Spirit, born of the Virgin Mary, suffered under Pontius Pilate, was crucified, died and was buried; he descended into hell; the third day, he rose again from the dead; he ascended into heaven and sits at the right hand of God, the Father almighty; from whence he shall come to judge the living and the dead. I believe in the Holy Spirit, the holy Catholic Church, the communion of saints, the forgiveness of sins, the resurrection of the body, and life everlasting. Amen.

Ad Nonam.

Deus in adiutorium meum intende: domine ad adiuuandum me festina. Gloria patri & filio ut supra.

Veni creator spiritus mentes tuorum visita: imple superna gratia que tu creasti pectora. Memento salutis auctor quod nostri quondam corporis ex illibata virgine nascendo formam sumpseris. Maria mater gratie mater misericordie tu nos ab ho-

Prayers before the First Mystery

Leader: Our Father, who art in heaven, hallowed be thy name. Thy kingdom come, thy will be done on earth as it is in heaven.

All: Give us this day our daily bread, and forgive us our trespasses as we forgive those who trespass against us. And lead us not into temptation but deliver us from evil. Amen.

Leader: Hail Mary, full of grace, the Lord is with thee. Blessed art thou among women and blessed is the fruit of thy womb, Jesus. (x 3)

All: Holy Mary, Mother of God, pray for us sinners, now and at the hour of our death. Amen. (x 3)

Leader: Glory be to the Father, and to the Son and to the Holy Spirit.

All: As it was in the beginning, is now and ever shall be, world without end. Amen.

The Joyful Mysteries

The angel said, 'Do not be afraid.
Look, I bring you news of great joy,
a joy to be shared by the whole people.'

Luke 1.73

The Word became flesh, he lived among us,
and we saw his glory, the glory that he has from the Father,
as only Son of the Father, full of grace and truth.

John 1.14

The Annunciation

Mary said, 'You see before you the Lord's servant, let it happen to me as you have said.' Luke 1.38

Leader: Our Father, who art in heaven, hallowed be thy name. Thy kingdom come, thy will be done on earth, as it is in heaven.

All: Give us this day our daily bread, and forgive us our trespasses, as we forgive those who trespass against us. And lead us not into temptation but deliver us from evil. Amen.

Leader: Hail Mary, full of grace, the Lord is with thee. Blessed art thou among women and blessed is the fruit of thy womb, Jesus. (x 10)

All: Holy Mary, Mother of God, pray for us sinners, now and at the hour of our death. Amen. (x 10)

Leader: Glory be to the Father, and to the Son and to the Holy Spirit.

All: As it was in the beginning, is now, and ever shall be, world without end. Amen.

The Visitation

Elizabeth gave a loud cry and said, 'Of all women you are the most blessed and blessed is the fruit of your womb. Why should I be honoured with a visit from the mother of my Lord?' Luke 1.42

Leader: Our Father, who art in heaven, hallowed be thy name. Thy kingdom come, thy will be done on earth, as it is in heaven.

All: Give us this day our daily bread, and forgive us our trespasses, as we forgive those who trespass against us. And lead us not into temptation but deliver us from evil. Amen.

Leader: Hail Mary, full of grace, the Lord is with thee. Blessed art thou among women and blessed is the fruit of thy womb, Jesus. (x 10)

All: Holy Mary, Mother of God, pray for us sinners, now and at the hour of our death. Amen. (x 10)

Leader: Glory be to the Father, and to the Son and to the Holy Spirit.

All: As it was in the beginning, is now, and ever shall be, world without end. Amen.

The Nativity

'Today in the town of David a Saviour has been born to you; he is Christ the Lord. And here is a sign for you: you will find a baby wrapped in swaddling clothes and lying in a manger.' Luke 2.11

Leader: Our Father, who art in heaven, hallowed be thy name. Thy kingdom come, thy will be done on earth, as it is in heaven.

All: Give us this day our daily bread, and forgive us our trespasses, as we forgive those who trespass against us. And lead us not into temptation but deliver us from evil. Amen.

Leader: Hail Mary, full of grace, the Lord is with thee. Blessed art thou among women and blessed is the fruit of thy womb, Jesus. (x 10)

All: Holy Mary, Mother of God, pray for us sinners, now and at the hour of our death. Amen. (x 10)

Leader: Glory be to the Father, and to the Son and to the Holy Spirit.

All: As it was in the beginning, is now, and ever shall be, world without end. Amen.

The Presentation of Jesus in the Temple

'Now Master, you are letting your servant go in peace as you have promised; for my eyes have seen the salvation which you have made ready in the sight of nations; a light of revelation for the Gentiles and glory for your people Israel.' Luke 2.29

Leader: Our Father, who art in heaven, hallowed be thy name. Thy kingdom come, thy will be done on earth, as it is in heaven.

All: Give us this day our daily bread, and forgive us our trespasses, as we forgive those who trespass against us. And lead us not into temptation but deliver us from evil. Amen.

Leader: Hail Mary, full of grace, the Lord is with thee. Blessed art thou among women and blessed is the fruit of thy womb, Jesus. (x 10)

All: Holy Mary, Mother of God, pray for us sinners, now and at the hour of our death. Amen. (x 10)

Leader: Glory be to the Father, and to the Son and to the Holy Spirit.

All: As it was in the beginning, is now, and ever shall be, world without end. Amen.

Finding the Child Jesus in the Temple

'Why were you looking for me? Did you not know that I must be in my Father's house?' Luke 2.49

Leader: Our Father, who art in heaven, hallowed be thy name. Thy kingdom come, thy will be done on earth, as it is in heaven.

All: Give us this day our daily bread, and forgive us our trespasses, as we forgive those who trespass against us. And lead us not into temptation but deliver us from evil. Amen.

Leader: Hail Mary, full of grace, the Lord is with thee. Blessed art thou among women and blessed is the fruit of thy womb, Jesus. (x 10)

All: Holy Mary, Mother of God, pray for us sinners, now and at the hour of our death. Amen. (x 10)

Leader: Glory be to the Father, and to the Son and to the Holy Spirit.

All: As it was in the beginning, is now, and ever shall be, world without end. Amen.

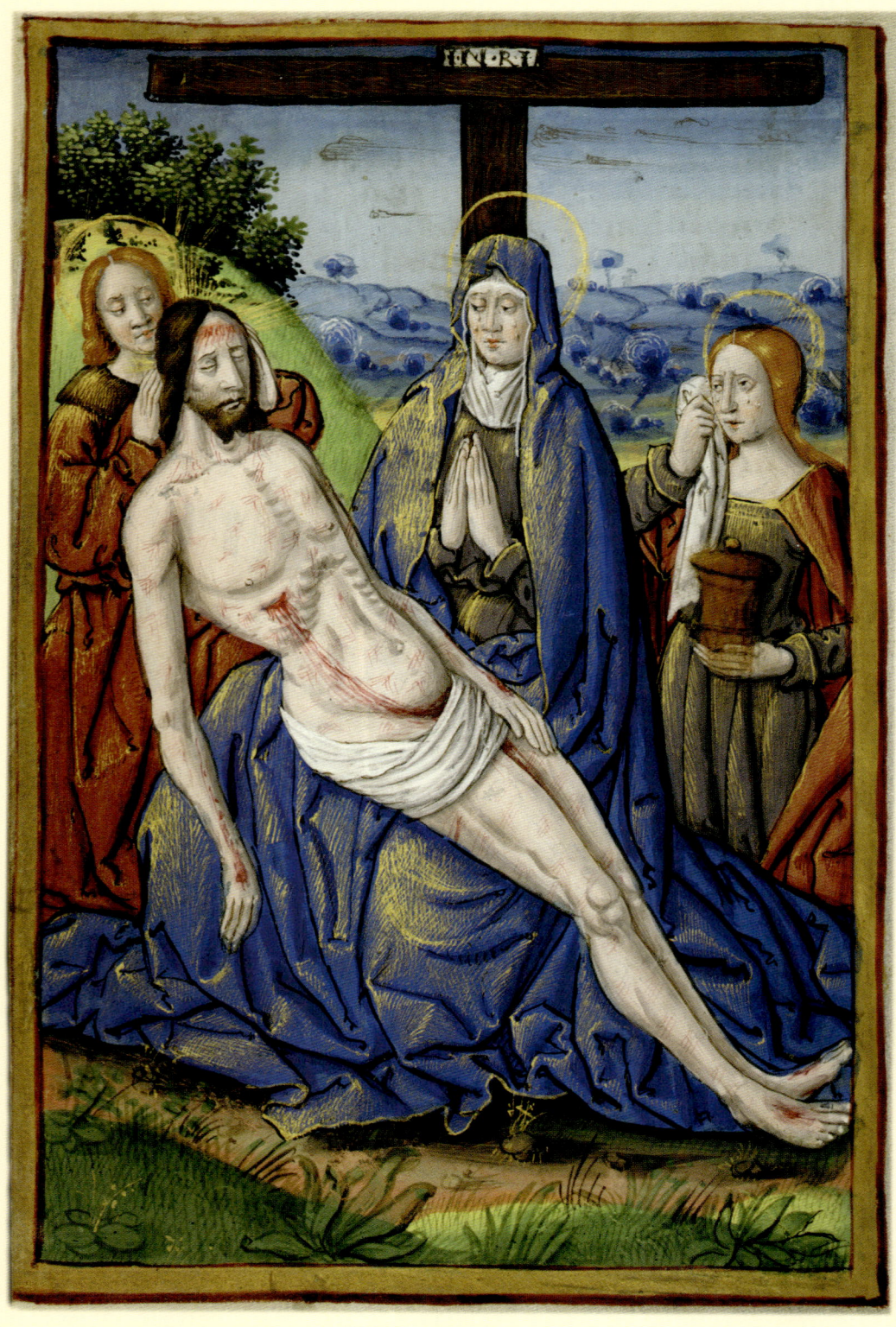

The Sorrowful Mysteries

*When the sixth hour came there was darkness
over the whole land until the ninth hour.
And at the ninth hour Jesus cried out in a loud voice,
'My God, my God why have you forsaken me?' ...
Jesus gave a loud cry and breathed his last.*

Mark 15.33

The Agony In The Garden

And going a little further he threw himself onto the ground and prayed that, if it were possible, this hour might pass him by. 'Father!' he said, 'for you everything is possible. Take this cup away from me. But let it be as you, not I, would have it.'   Mark 14.35

Leader: Our Father, who art in heaven, hallowed be thy name. Thy kingdom come, thy will be done on earth, as it is in heaven.

All: Give us this day our daily bread, and forgive us our trespasses, as we forgive those who trespass against us. And lead us not into temptation but deliver us from evil. Amen.

Leader: Hail Mary, full of grace, the Lord is with thee. Blessed art thou among women and blessed is the fruit of thy womb, Jesus. (x 10)

All: Holy Mary, Mother of God, pray for us sinners, now and at the hour of our death. Amen. (x 10)

Leader: Glory be to the Father, and to the Son and to the Holy Spirit.

All: As it was in the beginning, is now, and ever shall be, world without end. Amen.

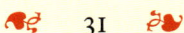

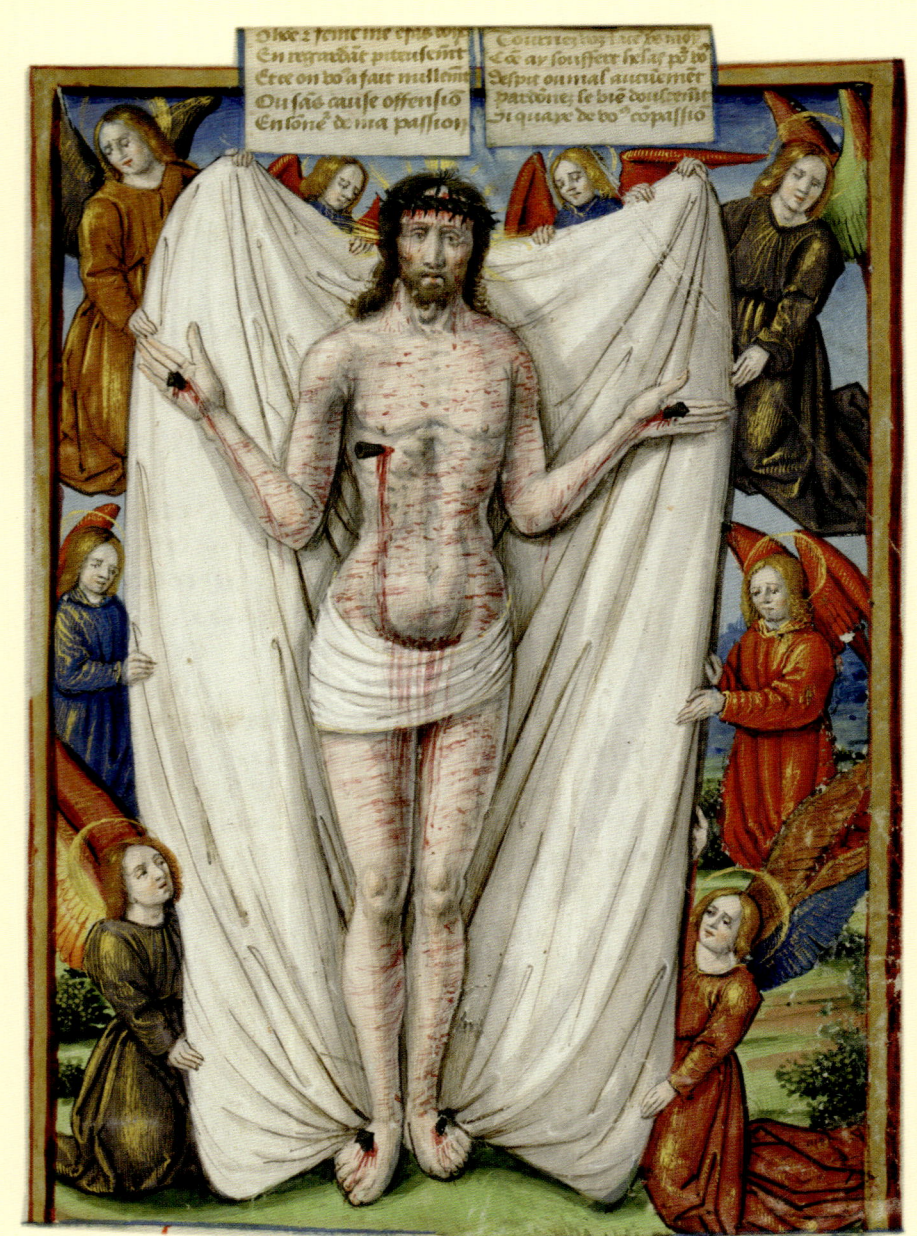

The Scourging at the Pillar

So Pilate, anxious to placate the crowd, released Barabbas for them, and after having Jesus scourged, he handed him over to be crucified.
Mark 15.15

Leader: Our Father, who art in heaven, hallowed be thy name. Thy kingdom come, thy will be done on earth, as it is in heaven.

All: Give us this day our daily bread, and forgive us our trespasses, as we forgive those who trespass against us. And lead us not into temptation but deliver us from evil. Amen.

Leader: Hail Mary, full of grace, the Lord is with thee. Blessed art thou among women and blessed is the fruit of thy womb, Jesus. (x 10)

All: Holy Mary, Mother of God, pray for us sinners, now and at the hour of our death. Amen. (x 10)

Leader: Glory be to the Father, and to the Son and to the Holy Spirit.

All: As it was in the beginning, is now, and ever shall be, world without end. Amen.

The Crowning with Thorns

And they stripped him and put a scarlet cloak round him, and having twisted some thorns into a crown they put this on his head and placed a reed in his right hand. To make fun of him they knelt to him saying, 'Hail, King of the Jews!' And they spat on him.   Matthew 27.29

Leader: Our Father, who art in heaven, hallowed be thy name. Thy kingdom come, thy will be done on earth, as it is in heaven.

All: Give us this day our daily bread, and forgive us our trespasses, as we forgive those who trespass against us. And lead us not into temptation but deliver us from evil. Amen.

Leader: Hail Mary, full of grace, the Lord is with thee. Blessed art thou among women and blessed is the fruit of thy womb, Jesus. (x 10)

All: Holy Mary, Mother of God, pray for us sinners, now and at the hour of our death. Amen. (x 10)

Leader: Glory be to the Father, and to the Son and to the Holy Spirit.

All: As it was in the beginning, is now, and ever shall be, world without end. Amen.

Jesus Carries His Cross

They then took charge of Jesus, and, carrying his own cross, he went out to the Place of the Skull, or, as it is called in Hebrew, Golgotha.   John 19.17

Leader: Our Father, who art in heaven, hallowed be thy name. Thy kingdom come, thy will be done on earth, as it is in heaven.

All: Give us this day our daily bread, and forgive us our trespasses, as we forgive those who trespass against us. And lead us not into temptation but deliver us from evil. Amen.

Leader: Hail Mary, full of grace, the Lord is with thee. Blessed art thou among women and blessed is the fruit of thy womb, Jesus. (x 10)

All: Holy Mary, Mother of God, pray for us sinners, now and at the hour of our death. Amen. (x 10)

Leader: Glory be to the Father, and to the Son and to the Holy Spirit.

All: As it was in the beginning, is now, and ever shall be, world without end. Amen.

The Crucifixion

Jesus cried out in a loud voice saying, 'Father, into your hands I commit my spirit.' With these words he breathed his last. Luke 23.46

Leader: Our Father, who art in heaven, hallowed be thy name. Thy kingdom come, thy will be done on earth, as it is in heaven.

All: Give us this day our daily bread, and forgive us our trespasses, as we forgive those who trespass against us. And lead us not into temptation but deliver us from evil. Amen.

Leader: Hail Mary, full of grace, the Lord is with thee. Blessed art thou among women and blessed is the fruit of thy womb, Jesus. (x 10)

All: Holy Mary, Mother of God, pray for us sinners, now and at the hour of our death. Amen. (x 10)

Leader: Glory be to the Father, and to the Son and to the Holy Spirit.

All: As it was in the beginning, is now, and ever shall be, world without end. Amen.

The Glorious Mysteries

And for this God raised him high
and gave him the name
which is above all other names;
so that all beings
in the heavens, on earth
and in the underworld,
should bend the knee at the name of Jesus
and that every tongue should acknowledge
Jesus Christ as Lord
to the glory of God the Father.

Phil. 2.9-11

The Resurrection

'Why look among the dead for someone who is alive? He is not here; he has risen.'   Luke 24.6

Leader: Our Father, who art in heaven, hallowed be thy name. Thy kingdom come, thy will be done on earth, as it is in heaven.

All: Give us this day our daily bread, and forgive us our trespasses, as we forgive those who trespass against us. And lead us not into temptation but deliver us from evil. Amen.

Leader: Hail Mary, full of grace, the Lord is with thee. Blessed art thou among women and blessed is the fruit of thy womb, Jesus. (x 10)

All: Holy Mary, Mother of God, pray for us sinners, now and at the hour of our death. Amen. (x 10)

Leader: Glory be to the Father, and to the Son and to the Holy Spirit.

All: As it was in the beginning, is now, and ever shall be, world without end. Amen.

The Ascension

He was lifted up while they looked on, and a cloud took him from their sight. They were still staring into the sky as he went, when suddenly two men in white were standing beside them and they said, 'Why are you Galileans standing here looking into the sky? This Jesus who has been taken from you into heaven will come back in the same way'. Acts 1.11

Leader: Our Father, who art in heaven, hallowed be thy name. Thy kingdom come, thy will be done on earth, as it is in heaven.

All: Give us this day our daily bread, and forgive us our trespasses, as we forgive those who trespass against us. And lead us not into temptation but deliver us from evil. Amen.

Leader: Hail Mary, full of grace, the Lord is with thee. Blessed art thou among women and blessed is the fruit of thy womb, Jesus. (x 10)

All: Holy Mary, Mother of God, pray for us sinners, now and at the hour of our death. Amen. (x 10)

Leader: Glory be to the Father, and to the Son and to the Holy Spirit.

All: As it was in the beginning, is now, and ever shall be, world without end. Amen.

The Descent of the Holy Spirit

When suddenly there came from heaven a sound as of a violent wind which filled the entire house in which they were sitting; and there appeared to them tongues as of fire; these separated and came to rest on the head of each of them. They were all filled with the Holy Spirit. Acts 2.3

Leader: Our Father, who art in heaven, hallowed be thy name. Thy kingdom come, thy will be done on earth, as it is in heaven.

All: Give us this day our daily bread, and forgive us our trespasses, as we forgive those who trespass against us. And lead us not into temptation but deliver us from evil. Amen.

Leader: Hail Mary, full of grace, the Lord is with thee. Blessed art thou among women and blessed is the fruit of thy womb, Jesus. (x 10)

All: Holy Mary, Mother of God, pray for us sinners, now and at the hour of our death. Amen. (x 10)

Leader: Glory be to the Father, and to the Son and to the Holy Spirit.

All: As it was in the beginning, is now, and ever shall be, world without end. Amen.

The Assumption of Our Lady

'My soul proclaims the greatness of the Lord, and my spirit rejoices in God my Saviour. He has looked upon his servant in her lowliness. Yes from now onwards all generations will call me blessed, for the Almighty has done great things for me' Luke 1.46

Leader: Our Father, who art in heaven, hallowed be thy name. Thy kingdom come, thy will be done on earth, as it is in heaven.

All: Give us this day our daily bread, and forgive us our trespasses, as we forgive those who trespass against us. And lead us not into temptation but deliver us from evil. Amen.

Leader: Hail Mary, full of grace, the Lord is with thee. Blessed art thou among women and blessed is the fruit of thy womb, Jesus. (x 10)

All: Holy Mary, Mother of God, pray for us sinners, now and at the hour of our death. Amen. (x 10)

Leader: Glory be to the Father, and to the Son and to the Holy Spirit.

All: As it was in the beginning, is now, and ever shall be, world without end. Amen.

Mary is crowned Queen of Heaven

Now a great sign appeared in heaven; a woman, robed with the sun, standing on the moon, and on her head a crown of twelve stars.
Revelation 12.1

Leader: Our Father, who art in heaven, hallowed be thy name. Thy kingdom come, thy will be done on earth, as it is in heaven.

All: Give us this day our daily bread, and forgive us our trespasses, as we forgive those who trespass against us. And lead us not into temptation but deliver us from evil. Amen.

Leader: Hail Mary, full of grace, the Lord is with thee. Blessed art thou among women and blessed is the fruit of thy womb, Jesus. (x 10)

All: Holy Mary, Mother of God, pray for us sinners, now and at the hour of our death. Amen. (x 10)

Leader: Glory be to the Father, and to the Son and to the Holy Spirit.

All: As it was in the beginning, is now, and ever shall be, world without end. Amen.

The Mysteries of Light

When Jesus spoke to the people again, he said

'I am the light of the world; anyone who follows me will not be walking in the dark, but will have the light of life.'

John 8.12

The Baptism of Jesus in the Jordan

And when Jesus had been baptised he at once came up from the water, and suddenly the heavens opened and he saw the Spirit of God descending like a dove and coming down on him. And suddenly there was a voice from heaven, 'This is my Son, the Beloved; my favour rests on him.' Matthew 3.16

Leader: Our Father, who art in heaven, hallowed be thy name. Thy kingdom come, thy will be done on earth, as it is in heaven.

All: Give us this day our daily bread, and forgive us our trespasses, as we forgive those who trespass against us. And lead us not into temptation but deliver us from evil. Amen.

Leader: Hail Mary, full of grace, the Lord is with thee. Blessed art thou among women and blessed is the fruit of thy womb, Jesus. (x 10)

All: Holy Mary, Mother of God, pray for us sinners, now and at the hour of our death. Amen. (x 10)

Leader: Glory be to the Father, and to the Son and to the Holy Spirit.

All: As it was in the beginning, is now, and ever shall be, world without end. Amen.

The Wedding at Cana

The mother of Jesus said to him, 'They have no wine.' Jesus said, 'Woman, what do you want from me? My hour has not yet come.' His mother said to the servants, 'Do whatever he tells you.'   John 2.3

Leader: Our Father, who art in heaven, hallowed be thy name. Thy kingdom come, thy will be done on earth, as it is in heaven.

All: Give us this day our daily bread, and forgive us our trespasses, as we forgive those who trespass against us. And lead us not into temptation but deliver us from evil. Amen.

Leader: Hail Mary, full of grace, the Lord is with thee. Blessed art thou among women and blessed is the fruit of thy womb, Jesus. (x 10)

All: Holy Mary, Mother of God, pray for us sinners, now and at the hour of our death. Amen. (x 10)

Leader: Glory be to the Father, and to the Son and to the Holy Spirit.

All: As it was in the beginning, is now, and ever shall be, world without end. Amen.

The Proclamation of the Kingdom

From then onwards Jesus began his proclamation with the message, 'Repent, for the kingdom of Heaven is close at hand.' Matthew 4.17

Leader: Our Father, who art in heaven, hallowed be thy name. Thy kingdom come, thy will be done on earth, as it is in heaven.

All: Give us this day our daily bread, and forgive us our trespasses, as we forgive those who trespass against us. And lead us not into temptation but deliver us from evil. Amen.

Leader: Hail Mary, full of grace, the Lord is with thee. Blessed art thou among women and blessed is the fruit of thy womb, Jesus. (x 10)

All: Holy Mary, Mother of God, pray for us sinners, now and at the hour of our death. Amen. (x 10)

Leader: Glory be to the Father, and to the Son and to the Holy Spirit.

All: As it was in the beginning, is now, and ever shall be, world without end. Amen.

The Transfiguration of Jesus

There in their presence he was transfigured: his face shone like the sun and his clothes became as dazzling as light. Suddenly from the cloud there came a voice which said, 'This is my Son, the Beloved; he enjoys my favour. Listen to him.'   Matthew 17.2 and 5

Leader: Our Father, who art in heaven, hallowed be thy name. Thy kingdom come, thy will be done on earth, as it is in heaven.

All: Give us this day our daily bread, and forgive us our trespasses, as we forgive those who trespass against us. And lead us not into temptation but deliver us from evil. Amen.

Leader: Hail Mary, full of grace, the Lord is with thee. Blessed art thou among women and blessed is the fruit of thy womb, Jesus. (x 10)

All: Holy Mary, Mother of God, pray for us sinners, now and at the hour of our death. Amen. (x 10)

Leader: Glory be to the Father, and to the Son and to the Holy Spirit.

All: As it was in the beginning, is now, and ever shall be, world without end. Amen.

The Institution of the Eucharist

Jesus took bread, and when he had said the blessing he broke it and gave it to the disciples. 'Take it and eat' he said, 'this is my body.' Then he took a cup and when he had given thanks he handed it to them saying, 'Drink from this, all of you, for this is my blood, the blood of the covenant, poured out for many for the forgiveness of sins.' Matthew 26.26

Leader: Our Father, who art in heaven, hallowed be thy name. Thy kingdom come, thy will be done on earth, as it is in heaven.

All: Give us this day our daily bread, and forgive us our trespasses, as we forgive those who trespass against us. And lead us not into temptation but deliver us from evil. Amen.

Leader: Hail Mary, full of grace, the Lord is with thee. Blessed art thou among women and blessed is the fruit of thy womb, Jesus. (x 10)

All: Holy Mary, Mother of God, pray for us sinners, now and at the hour of our death. Amen. (x 10)

Leader: Glory be to the Father, and to the Son and to the Holy Spirit.

All: As it was in the beginning, is now, and ever shall be, world without end. Amen.

Prayers after the Rosary

All: Hail, Holy Queen, Mother of Mercy, hail our life our sweetness and our hope. To thee do we cry, poor banished children of Eve, to thee do we send up our sighs, mourning and weeping in this vale of tears. Turn then, most gracious advocate, thine eyes of mercy upon us, and, after this our exile, show unto us the blessed fruit of thy womb, Jesus; O clement, O loving, O sweet Virgin Mary.

Leader: Pray for us, O Holy Mother of God.

All: That we may be made worthy of the promises of Christ.

Leader: Let us pray.

All: O God, whose only begotten Son, by his life, death and resurrection has purchased for us the rewards of eternal life, grant we beseech thee, that meditating on these Mysteries of the Most Holy Rosary of the Blessed Virgin Mary, we may both imitate what they contain and obtain what they promise, through the same Christ our Lord, Amen.

Leader: May the Divine Assistance remain always with us.

All: And may the souls of the faithful departed, through the mercy of God, rest in peace. Amen.

All: In the name of the Father, and of the Son and of the Holy Spirit. Amen.

Prayers from Primers

THUS FAR, MOST OF THE ILLUSTRATIONS have come from hand written illuminated manuscripts, Books of Hours, valued both for the prayers they contained and the status they bestowed on the owner; few could afford them. They were almost always in Latin.

Printing brought about a great expansion in the numbers of Books of Hours, or Primers. Their relative cheapness meant that they found a new market with those who could not afford luxurious illuminated manuscripts.

Prayers in English first appeared in the 1490s, and although traditional prayers in the new printed Primers remained in Latin, increasing numbers were printed in the vernacular. Those reproduced here come from two Primers in the Sarum, or Salisbury, rite, of 1516 and 1541. They reflect the concerns of their day, in many ways universal to all times – a longing for salvation, pleas for deliverance from sin and temptation, and a deep devotion to Christ and his Mother. The language varies from the simple to the near metaphysical, with the picturesque description of the weight of sin as 'heaviness' on the soul, and the literal translation of the Amen into the more affirmative English, 'So be it'.

VIRGIN MOTHER of the congregation
Gate of Glory that never is done
Be for us a reconciliation
Unto the father and the son.

Sarum Primer 1516

GLORYE BE to God the Father
Glorye to Chryste that made us free
Glorye also to the Holy Comforter
One God and persons three.
So be it.

Sarum Primer 1516

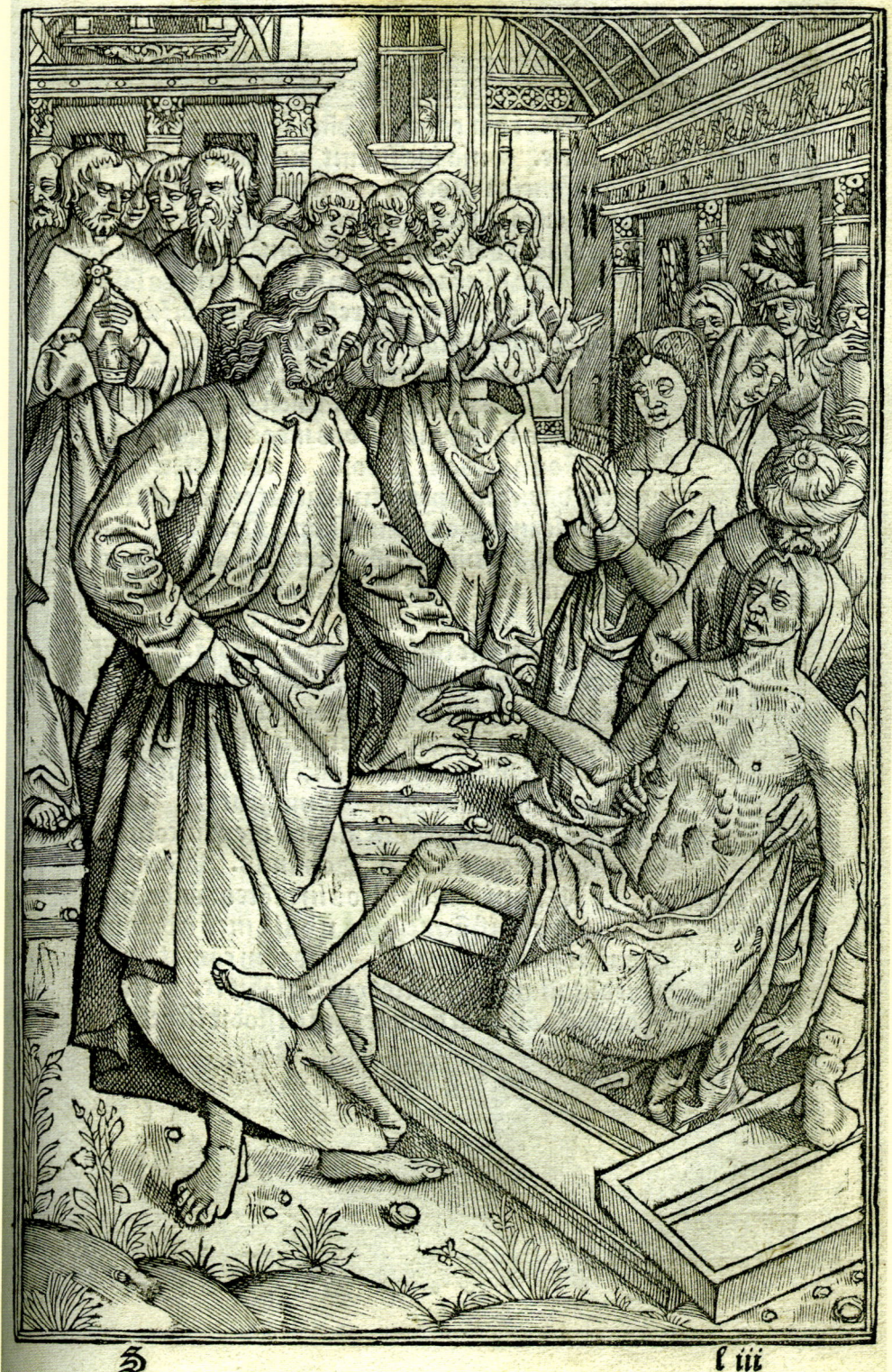

l iii

TO THE LORD we commend the souls of thy servants, both men and women, so that they being dead to the world may live to thee, and all the sins that they have committed by the frailty of worldly conversation, Thou Lord wash away by the forgiveness of thy most merciful Pity.
By Christ our Lord
God have mercy on all Christian souls.
So be it.

Sarum Primer 1541

For a Competence of Living

TWO THINGS Lorde I demand of thee that thou wouldst not deny me until I die. Vanity and worde of lying make far from me.
Poverty or riches give me not.
Only give that is necessary for my living, lest perchance being in full abundance I might be provoked to deny thee and say 'Who is Lord?' Or compelled by necessity I might steal and so forswear the name of my God.
So be it.

Sarum Primer 1516

Hymne

HAYLE STARRE of the sea most radiant
O mother of God most glorious
A pure virgin always persevering
O gate of heaven most gorgeous
Thou was saluted with great humilitie when
Gabriel said Ave Maria
Establysshe us in peace and tranquilitie
And change the name of sinful Eve
Loose the prisoners from captivitie
Unto the blynde give sighte agayne
Deliver us from our malignitye
To the ende we may some grace attayne.

Sarum Primer 1516

The passyon. Fo. viii.

for the ¶ pached euery where. And the lorde wrought wicche the͂/⁊ cōfirmed the worde with myracles that folowed ¶ The passid wrytten by sayne Iohan.

dn̄s cooperāte ⁊ sermonē confirmante seq̄tib⁹ signis. b. g̊. Paulo d̄i n̄ri eccl̄ie secūdū Iohāṅ.

Whan Iesus had spoken these wordes/he wēt forthe with his ⁊ disciples ouer the brokeced͂zō where

Egressus est d̄ñs Iesus cum discipulis suis trans torrentē cedron vbi erat

THE GLORIOUS passion of our lord
Jesus Christe
Deliver us from sorrow and heaviness
And bring us to the joys of Paradise.
So be it.

Sarum Primer 1516

GRAUNT, WE BESECHE thee Lord God
that thy servauntes may ennjoye
contynuall helthe of body & soule
And thorough the gracious intercessyon
of the Virgyn thy mother
that we may be delyvered from
this present hevynes
and to have the fruycyon of eternall gladnes.
By Chryst our Lorde.
Blesse we the Lorde.
Thanke we God.

Sarum Primer 1516

Stonyhurst College

STONYHURST COLLEGE WAS FOUNDED in 1593 by an English Jesuit, Fr Robert Persons. Elizabethan laws made it illegal for a Catholic school to exist in England, so it was established at St Omer, now in Northern France, and remained on the Continent until the French Revolution forced it to seek sanctuary in Lancashire in 1794. From its foundation it was regarded by English Catholics as a safe haven, not only for their sons, but also for precious religious books, manuscripts, vestments, church plate and relics which were incriminating possessions in 17th century England. Many such were sent across the seas to St Omer. These now form the nucleus of the College's present day collection of pre and post Reformation Catholic artefacts, held in trust by the Jesuits, and used today to inspire and educate new generations. This book arose out of an educational project involving two pupils at the College.

Today, Stonyhurst College is a co-educational boarding and day school in the Jesuit tradition. The Libraries, Collections and Archives are available for schools, groups and academics to view by appointment. For more information please contact the Curator.

BOOKS OF HOURS

Books of Hours were intended for use by pious lay people to enable them to join in the prayers said in monastic communities without having to take religious vows. They were immensely popular from about the 12th century to the 16th century.

The books came in a wide variety of styles and quality – from the richest book with gold leaf and lapis lazuli paints to plain unadorned texts. They could be bought off the shelf from book shops, or specially commissioned to suit the individual's needs and pocket from a workshop or monastic scriptorium. There was great demand for these books, and a thriving second hand trade grew up. Many are inscribed with the names of different owners over a period of several hundred years – proof of the durable nature of these books and the esteem in which they were held.

Illustration: front cover of Ms 65, Preces Variae, c1500

HOW BOOKS OF HOURS WERE USED

Most Books of Hours follow a similar pattern: at the beginning is a calendar with the feasts of the Church. The major feasts were often illuminated in red ink – the so called 'red letter days'. The Gospel, Office of Our Lady, Seven Penitential Psalms, and the Office for the Dead were always included. Other psalms, readings, masses and prayers could be added according to local custom or individual specification.

The Office of Our Lady consisted of eight episodes in Mary's life, allowing the person praying to intercede for Mary's help through contemplating her life, and that of her son – rather like the rosary. The eight episodes were prayed at specific hours, echoing the practice of monastic communities, starting with Matins before dawn through to Compline in the late evening. Intercessions for deceased family members and friends were offered daily through recital of the Office for the Dead – a very important part of medieval prayer life.

Illustration: Calendar of Feast Days for March, Book of Hours printed in London 1512.

THE PRODUCTION OF ILLUMINATED MANUSCRIPTS

Manuscript simply means 'handwritten'. Most Books of Hours are decorated with miniature pictures, foliage borders or decorated initial letters, which are known as illuminations. Originally these manuscripts were produced in monastic scriptoria, or writing workshops. In the 13th century lay workshops appeared, and soon had taken over most of the production of Books of Hours and other popular devotional manuscripts. The French and Flemish workshops were the most prolific and prestigious. Most workshops worked anonymously – very few manuscripts are signed.

Manuscript pages are invariably made from vellum – calf, goat or sheep skin scraped, treated with lime and stretched. It is very durable, and high quality vellum gives a smooth shiny surface ideal for painting and gilding. Once prepared, the animal skins were cut into sheets and hand ruled ready for writing. To save time, some sheets were pricked through several thicknesses with a tool that marked where the lines were to be drawn. These small holes are visible on many manuscripts.

Illustration: Initial letter D. MS 57 *Wolsey Book of Hours,* Flemish c 1400.

INK, PIGMENT AND GOLD LEAF

Medieval scribes used goose or swan quills for writing, sharpened up to sixty times in a working day. The ink was thicker than that we use today, and was made from a mixture of lamp blacking or charcoal, mixed with gum for black ink, or by boiling the oak 'apples' created by gall wasps and adding ferrous sulphate and gum – this produced a browner, softer colour.

Pigments, too, were prepared as needed. Many were based on vegetable or animal by-products, and some, such as vermilion, which was made from mercury and sulphur, were highly toxic. The most prized of all pigments was ultramarine. This clear bright blue paint was made by grinding lapis lazuli from Afghanistan and mixing it with binding agents. It cost more than gold, and was reserved for only the most expensive books – it was also the colour usually used for Mary's robes.

Gold leaf appears in many of the finer Books of Hours. Pure gold sheets were cut and applied onto a sticky gesso base then burnished. Sometimes the gesso was built up into a thick layer, giving a three dimensional effect. Gold dust was also mixed with gum to give a paint which produced a sugary, sparkly effect.

Illustration: MS 33, Heures de Nostre Dame, French, Use of Paris c1430.

HEURES DE NOSTRE DAME
MS 33

This beautifully illuminated manuscript has 178 leaves of vellum, every page highly decorated. It contains miscellaneous prayers, the Office of Our Lady, the Penitential Psalms, the Litany, Offices of the Holy Cross, the Holy Spirit and the Dead, the fifteen Joys of Our Lady, the five Wounds of Our Lord and the Mass of Our Lady.

It was made in France around 1430, and uses the rite common in Paris. There are no inscriptions to identify its original owner, but her portrait appears on folio 159, praying in front of the Virgin and Child. Judging by the high quality of the illuminations in the book she commissioned, she must have been wealthy. Portraits such as these were common; the person paying for the book wishes to record her piety for posterity, and also to encourage other, later, readers to remember her in their prayers.

Illustration: Lady praying in front of Virgin and Child, f159r.

THE HOURS OF
ELIZABETH PLANTAGENET
MS 37

An inscription at the back of this book – 'Elizabeth Plantagenet the Quene' – identifies it as the property of Elizabeth of York, wife of Henry VII. Elizabeth became queen in 1486, and died in childbirth on her 37th birthday in 1503. The book itself dates from 1475-1500. The ownership inscription was written on two different occasions. The first part, *Elizabeth Plantagenet*, dates from the time she received the book, before her marriage to Henry VII. Later, after her coronation, she inscribed the words, *the Quene*, after her name.

There are 197 vellum leaves and 21 full page miniatures. The lavish use of ultramarine and gold dust pigment marks it out as a valuable possession. In addition to the usual Calendar, Penitential Psalms, Offices of Our Lady and the Dead, it contains miniatures of Saints Peter and Paul, St Sebastian, St Nicholas and St Catherine. These would have had personal significance for the original owner of the book.

Illustration: The Archangel Michael vanquishing Satan, f191r.

PRECES VARIAE
MS 45

The title of this manuscript means 'Various Prayers', and among the usual Offices and psalms, it contains the Mass for the Holy Relics of the Royal Chapel in Paris – the Sainte Chapelle. This chapel contained the rich collection of relics amassed by the French Royal Family since the 13th century. They included, amongst many others, the Crown of Thorns, a spine from which was given to Mary Queen of Scots and is now at Stonyhurst College.

The book dates from 1500-1510 and has 63 miniatures of the highest quality. There is another very similar manuscript now in the Louvre in Paris, and it is accepted that both books were produced for the use of the French Royal Family in the Sainte Chapelle.

The illustration shows the Miraculous Mass of St Gregory the Great. The 7th century Pope prayed for a miracle after being confronted with a parishioner who refused to believe that the Eucharist was truly the Body of Christ. During the Mass, the image of Christ and the instruments of the Passion appeared on the altar.

Illustration: The Mass of St Gregory, f65r.

THE HOURS OF KATHERINE BRAY
MS 60

This book belonged to Katherine Bray, wife of Sir Reginald Bray. Sir Reginald was a close friend of Henry VII, and was the soldier who reputedly found Richard III's crown on Bosworth Field. He was also the architect of Henry VII's chapel in Westminster Abbey, where Elizabeth Plantagenet is buried. Katherine Bray was a lady in waiting to Queen Elizabeth.

An inscription on folio 104 asks the reader to pray for Katherine's soul and that of John Colet, Dean of St Paul's, and close friend of St Thomas More. We presume that the book passed to John Colet on Katherine's death, and the unknown scribe wished readers to pray for both their souls after Colet's death in 1519. The illuminations are attributed to the Flemish Master of the Hortulus Animae, who was working between 1480-90. He adopted the technique of painting realistic flowery borders, and many of his miniatures, such as this one, are painted in grisaille – a monochrome scheme intended to resemble sculpted reliefs.

Illustration: The Raising of Lazarus, f104v.

THE HOURS OF MADELEINE LEVESQUE
MS 59

Madeleine Levesque inscribed her name in this book in 1636, although the manuscript dates from c1480. Sadly, we know nothing about her other than her name, but it is obvious that the book was still being used for devotions 150 years after it was first written.

The illuminations are attributed to a French artist known only as Maitre François. Manuscript work was very lucrative, and many artists worked solely on producing illustrations for Books of Hours. As so many of these contained standard images, such as the Nativity or the Crucifixion, these illuminations could be produced *en masse* and were sent on to the retailers of Books of Hours, known as stationers, who collated the images with the text, bound them and sold them.

This graphic image of a burial service comes from the Office of the Dead, and is a reminder of the constant fear of unexpected death without receiving the last sacraments in the medieval period. It was seen as being very important to pray for the dead, interceding for a lessening of their time in Purgatory.

Illustration: Mass for the Burial of the Dead, f50r.

THE HOURS OF CARDINAL WOLSEY
MS 57

An inscription on the flyleaf of this manuscript states that it was a gift to Cardinal Wolsey from the Papal Legate, Cardinal Campeggio, who visited England in 1528-9 to hear the case of Henry VIII's divorce from Catherine of Aragon. The inscription probably dates from the 17th century, but that doesn't mean that the claim is invalid, simply that a later owner decided to record a long standing tradition that the book was Wolsey's. The book was rebound in the 17th century, and the pages trimmed, obliterating some of the illumination.

The book dates from around 1400. The miniatures are Flemish and the decorative borders English. The calendar lists English saints, so it was intended for use in this country. In addition to the usual contents, the Psalter of Jerome is included. St Jerome was the greatest translator of the Bible and Psalms in the history of the Church. He is shown here with a quill, and his lion companion – supposedly befriended when Jerome was a hermit in the desert. In fact the lion really belonged to St Gerasius, but an early medieval mistranslation bestowed him on Jerome, and he has been portrayed with a lion ever since.

Illustration: St Jerome with his lion, f158v.

PRINTED BOOKS OF HOURS

By the beginning of the 16th century there had grown an international trade in printed Books of Hours. The publishers of Paris cornered much of the market, but sent a good deal of work to their sister printing houses in London. The versatility of the printing process allowed the trade to produce editions of books tailored for different countries and dioceses, but the mass production method largely precluded individually commissioned books.

The speed at which large numbers of books could be produced cut costs dramatically, as did the fact that they were largely printed on paper and not the more expensive vellum. Woodcut illustrations were cheap to produce and were reused over decades. Printed Books of Hours became affordable to all but the poorest and at the start of the Reformation in Europe were the most popular books available.

Illustration: Death and the Jester. Book of Hours printed by Simon Vostre, 1512, f1.

HOURS OF THE VIRGIN

Printed by Simon Vostre, Paris 1512

The publishing house of Simon Vostre on the Rue Neuve Notre Dame produced some of the most lavishly illustrated and best known Books of Hours of his day. His books mixed late Gothic and Renaissance styles to great effect, and he endlessly reused his illustrations.

Vostre employed the best printmakers available, and reworked prints by Durer and other famous contemporary artists. Durer was not amused when others plagiarised his work, and became the first artist to invoke a form of copyright.

The success of the early printed books of hours led to a profusion of printing houses producing these and other books of devotions, such as the *Rosarium Mysticum* also reproduced in this book.

Illustration: Press mark from Book of Hours, 1520

ILLUSTRATIONS

2   *Frontispiece*: Lady praying in front of Virgin and Child MS 33, *Heures de Nostre Dame*, c 1430
6   The Madonna and Child with the Holy Trinity and Saints MS 45, *Preces Variae*, c 1500
10 Gilt rosary, 18th century
12 Angels Praising the Trinity MS 45, *Preces Variae*, c 1500
14 Prayers for Terce MS 60, *The Hours of Katherine Bray*, c 1410
16 Madonna and Child MS 60, *The Hours of Katherine Bray*, c 1410
18 The Annunciation MS 33, *Heures de Nostre Dame*, c 1430
20 The Visitation MS 59, *Hours of Madeleine Levesque*, c 1480
22 The Angels bring the Good News to the Shepherds MS 59, *Hours of Madeleine Levesque*, c 1480
24 The Presentation MS 37, *Plantagenet Hours*, c 1475
26 Mary with the Child Jesus MS 45, *Preces Variae*, c 1500
28 Pieta MS 45, *Preces Variae*, c 1500
30 Jesus prays in the Garden of Gethsemane MS 57, *Wolsey Hours*, c 1410
32 The Wounds of Christ – The Pity MS 45, *Preces Variae*, c 1500
34 The Crowning with Thorns MS 45, *Preces Variae*, c 1500
36 Detail from Scenes of the Passion MS 45, *Preces Variae*, c 1500
38 Crucifixion with the Virgin and St John MS 33, *Heures de Nostre Dame*, c 1430
40 Pentecost MS 59, *Hours of Madeleine Levesque*, c 1480
42 The Resurrection MS 45, *Preces Variae*, c 1500
44 Angels adoring the Trinity MS 45, *Preces Variae*, c 1500
46 Mary and the Apostles at Pentecost MS 45, *Preces Variae*, c 1500
48 Virgin in Prayer MS 45, *Preces Variae*, c 1500
50 The Coronation of the Virgin MS 37, *Plantagenet Hours*, c 1475
52 The Angel brings the Good News to the Shepherds MS 60, *Hours of Katherine Bray*, 1480-90
54 The Baptism of Christ *Rosarium Mysticum*, Antwerp 1533
56 Fons Pietatis MS 45, *Preces Variae*, c 1500
58 Jesus Preaching MS 45, *Preces Variae*, c 1500
60 The Transfiguration *Book of Hours* printed by Simon Vostre, Paris 1512
62 The Miraculous Mass of St Gregory MS 45, *Preces Variae*, c 1500
64 Prayers for Terce MS 60, *Hours of Katherine Bray*, c 1480
66 The Tree of Jesse *Book of Hours* printed by Simon Vostre, Paris 1512
68 The Annunciation *Book of Hours* printed by Simon Vostre, Paris 1512
70 The Blessed Virgin before the Holy Trinity *Rosarium Mysticum*, Antwerp 1533
72 The Raising of Lazarus *Book of Hours* printed by Simon Vostre, Paris 1512
74 July *Sarum Primer* 1516
76 The Madonna and Child in Glory before the Pope and the Holy Roman Emperor *Rosarium Mysticum*, 1533
78 The Crucifixion *Sarum Primer*, 1516
80 The Coronation of the Virgin *Book of Hours* printed by Simon Vostre, Paris 1512
82 The West Front, Stonyhurst

LDS

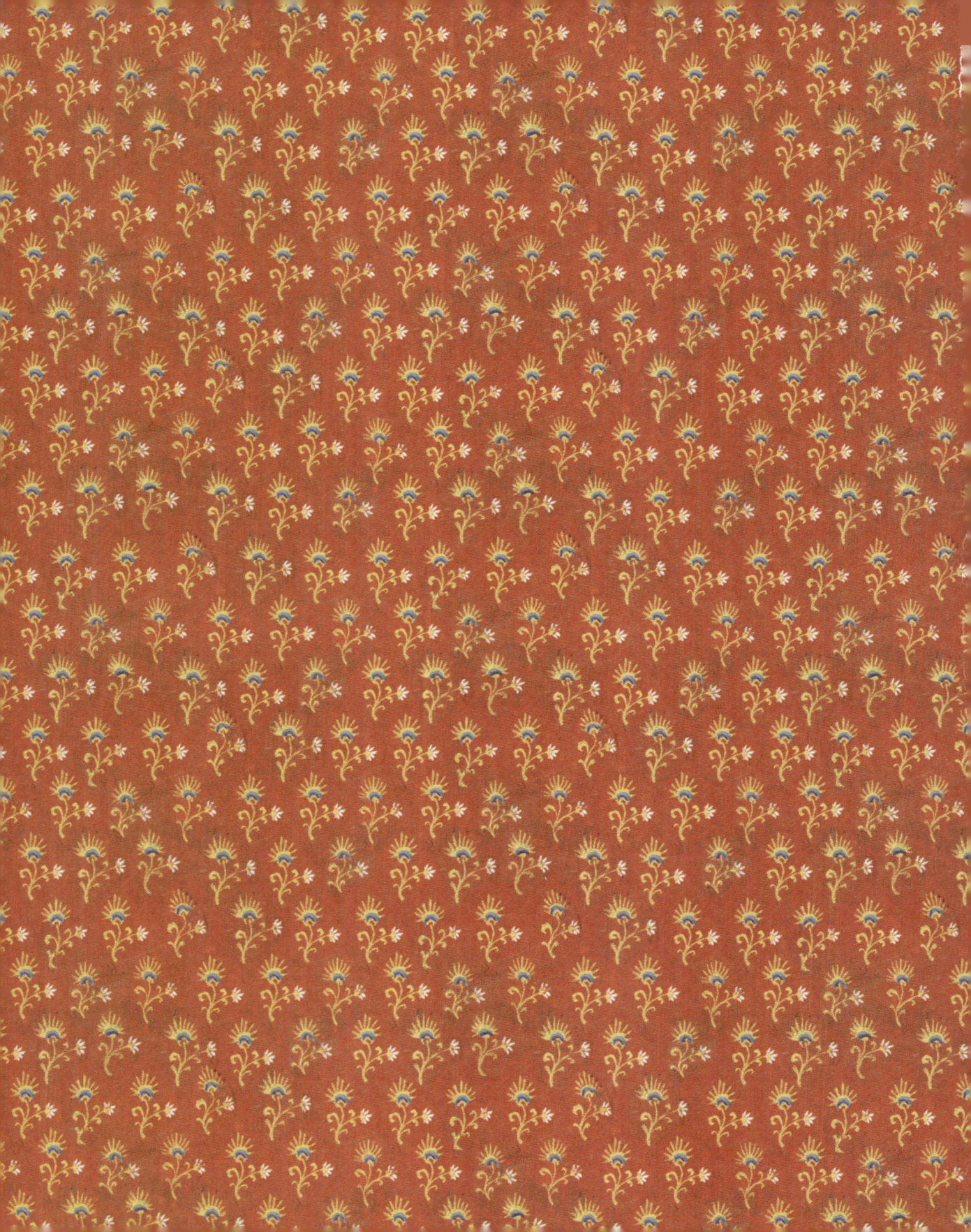